VISION AND COMPREHENSION OF
STRASBOURG

Idea and photography by the Editions MAGE team.

Photographs: Robert Klingelschmitt, John F. Linares, Jean-Louis Lagrange, James Paulmier.

Texts: Robert Klingelschmitt and James Paulmier.

Copyright of this edition for photographs and text: © EDITORIAL ESCUDO DE ORO, S.A. - Palaudarias, 26 - 08004 Barcelona (Spain) - Editions MAGE : 19, rue Albert Einstein, Lot 16 - 93591 LE BLANC-MESNIL CEDEX.
Tel: 16 (1) 48-65-53-20.

4th Edition

I.S.B.N. 84-378-1261-5

Dep. Legal B. 24899-1997

Printed in the EEC

Front cover: typical roofs and cathedral. The Alsace escutcheon, and the colours of Europe.

STRASBOURG

0 100   500 m.

N

Panoramic view of Strasbourg. Vauban Dam and the Covered Bridges are in the foreground, the cathedral is in the background.

STRASBOURG, CAPITAL OF EUROPE

STRASBOURG, CAPITAL OF ALSACE

''How beautiful is our Alsace'' goes the popular song...

This beauty, along with the natural wealth and resources, has made Alsace a coveted region for over two thousand years.

Strasbourg took root in this legendary soil, the cradle of Rhine civilization. Various ordeals over the centuries have blunted neither the wisdom nor the friendliness of native Alsatians so strongly attached to their traditions and to their land. With such strong roots, Strasbourg has been able to grow and assume a regional and national role, its influence extending not only to Europe but to the world.

Strasbourg started out as a small fishing village inhabited by the Triboque tribe, situated on a piece of land surrounded by marshes and bordered by the twin branches of the river Ill, a tributary of the Rhine. In 61 B.C. the Suevians, a Germanic tribe, crossed the Rhine.

Julius Caesar's legions promptly inflicted a stunning defeat, and then proceeded to install themselves in Alsace for the next five hundred years. They established military outposts throughout the region, one of them becoming a ''castrum'' or garrison town known as Argentorate. In 355 A.D., the Alemans captured the town.

But by 357 the Alemans were defeated by the troops of Emperor Julian the Apostate on Strasbourg plain. In 451, the city was conquered and razed by the Huns.

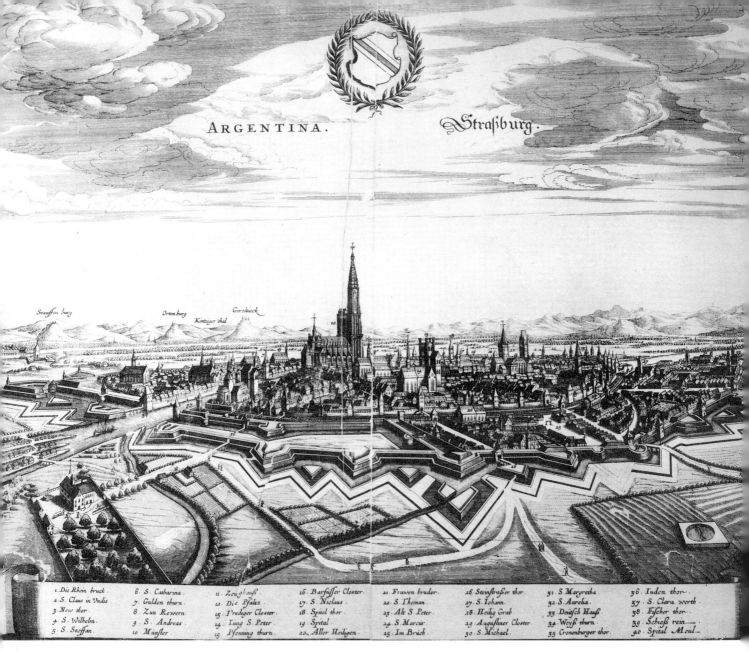

ARGENTINA.   Straßburg.

Stauffen burg   Orten burg   Gerstueck
                          Kintziger thal

1. Die Rhein bruck.	6. S. Catharina.	11. Zeughauß.	16. Barfuffer Closter.	21. Frawen bruder.	26. Steinftraßer thor.	31. S. Margretha.	36. Iuden thor.
2. S. Claus in Vndis.	7. Gulden thurn.	12. Die Pfaltz.	17. S. Niclaus.	22. S. Thoman.	27. S. Iohann.	32. S. Aurelia.	37. S. Clara werth.
3. New thor.	8. Zun Rewern.	13. Prediger Closter.	18. Spitel thor.	23. Alt S. Peter.	28. Heilig Grab.	33. Doitfch Hauß.	38. Fifcher thor.
4. S. Wilhelm.	9. S. Andreas.	14. Iung S. Peter.	19. Spital.	24. S. Marcur.	29. Augustiner Closter.	34. Weyß thurn.	39. Scheß rein.
5. S. Stoffan.	10. Munfter.	15. Pfenning thurn.	20. Aller Heiligen.	25. Im Bruch.	30. S. Michael.	35. Cronenburger thor.	40. Spital Meul.

General view from the North-East. Engraving by Mathieu Merian for his album entitled Topographia Alsatiae
(1644).

The town finally assumed the Germanic name of ''Strateburgum'' (''the town by the roads'') after Clovis' victory at Tolbiac.
Strasbourg thus became the hub of the road and river network, the centre of commercial transactions between the Mediterranean and northern Europe.

It was in Strasbourg on February 14, 842, during the declining Carolingian empire, that Louis the German and Charles the Bald took the well-known ''Oath of Strasbourg'', which today represents the oldest document in the Romance and Teutonic languages. They thereby swore allegiance against their older

Raven Court. Lithograph by Samuel Prout (circa 1824).

Mercière Street, with a fine view of the cathedral façade. Lithograph by Chapuy.

brother Lothar, although it was Lothar who was awarded Alsace and Strasbourg in the treaty of Verdun the following year.

Following the death of Lothar II, the country reverted to Louis the German in 855 and remained part of the Germanic Holy Roman Empire until the treaty of Westphalia (1648). The Bishop governed the city with extensive imperial powers that went beyond those of the secular lords, including the right to mete out high justice.

In 1262, local notables and guild corporations formed a militia. The episcopal troops of Walter Von Géroldseck, Bishop of Strasbourg, were defeated at Hausbergen. Strasbourg thus became a City of the Empire, with the right to coin money, sign treaties, and promulgate laws.

Taking advantage of a feud between two clans of nobles —the Zorn and Mullenheim families— city craftsmen and guilds seized the keys to the city and proclaimed the ''Strasbourg Republic'' in 1332. The commoners were represented in the council by twenty five representatives. The true head of the city was the Ammeister, who represented the corporations and craft guilds. The people swore allegiance to him every year. In 1334, a charter (Schwörbrief) formally ratified the municipal constitution.

It was during the 15th century that Strasbourg gained the reputation as one of Europe's most beautiful cities. In addition to completing the cathedral (1439) and installing a Gutenberg type printing press (1434-1444), its artistic influence was such that Strasbourg was both crossroads and midwife to the New Ideas promoted by the first generation of humanists (Sebastian Brandt, Wimpheling...).

As of 1518, the population was divided over the issue of the reformation. The city council decided to break with the Church of Rome.

The Thirty Years War (1618-1648) was perhaps the

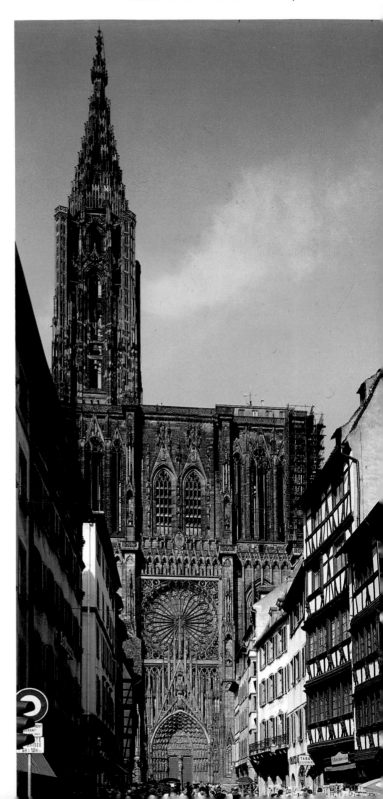

The nave, begun in the 13th century, has seven bays and is 32 metres high.

severest trial in the history of Alsace. According to the treaty of Westphalia, in 1648, freedom of religion is again guaranteed and the Emperor must cede Alsace to France. Yet Strasbourg hangs on to its independence, remaining a City of the Empire. It is subsequently encircled by 30,000 men under the command of Louvois, Louis XIV's minister of war. A surrender agreement was signed on September 30, 1681, enabling King Louis XIV to make a solemn entry into the city on October 23.

Strasbourg thus became a "Free Royal City", keeping its rights and customs. The cathedral once again become Catholic. The city accepted a garrison of French troops, as well as a Representative of the Crown and a Royal Administrator. It continued to coin its own money, and German remained the administrative language.

The people rose up during the French revolution, occupying the former Town Hall on July 19, 1789. And it was at Strasbourg, on April 25, 1792, that Cap-

tain Rouget de l'Isle composed a battle song for the Rhine Army spread across the country and became the national anthem "La Marseillaise".

During the First Empire, two people from Strasbourg —Kléber and Kellermann— distinguished themselves on the battlefield. A period of rapid growth followed the signing of the peace treaty of 1815.

In 1870, beseiged and bombarded by the Germans, the city was forced to capitulate on September 28. Alsace and Lorraine were annexed and remained under German domination until November 22, 1918. On June 19, 1940, German troops once again occupied the city, remaining there until Field Marshal Leclerc liberated it on November 23, 1944.

Strasbourg is today an urban community of nearly 400,000 inhabitants, and hosts a university counting 33,000 students. It is the seat of the Council of Europe and of the European Commission and Court of Human Rights, as well housing the European Parliament: a truly modern city of international scope.

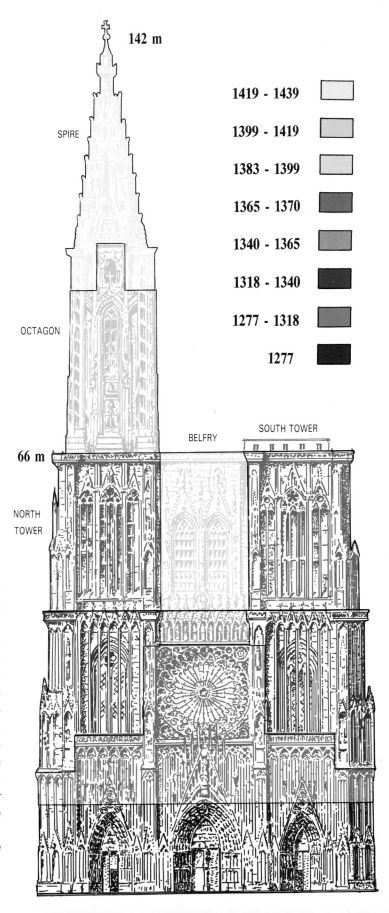

Notre-Dame Cathedral.

142 m

SPIRE

OCTAGON

66 m

NORTH
TOWER

BELFRY

SOUTH TOWER

1419 - 1439

1399 - 1419

1383 - 1399

1365 - 1370

1340 - 1365

1318 - 1340

1277 - 1318

1277

NOTRE-DAME CATHEDRAL

A magnificent jewel of pink sandstone quarried in the Vosges mountains, overlooking old Strasbourg, Notre Dame cathedral was originally the site of a primitive, roman-style cathedral begun in 1015 by Bishop Wernher of Hapsburg. It required 37 years to complete. Throughout the 12th century the cathedral was ravaged by a number of fires. Beginning in 1176 successive generations of builders labored for 163 years to produce the monument that still stands today. The new builders built on the framework of the Romanesque cathedral and kept the same dimensions. Bishop Conrad of Hüneburg decided to rebuild the east part where elements of the Romanesque style can be observed. Already apparent, however, was the influence of Gothic art, in full bloom as early as 1235 in the construction of the main nave with its ribbed vaults, its slender clustered columns, and its polychrome stained glass windows, and triumphant after 1284 in the splendid western façade thanks to the genius of Erwin of Steinbach. In 1365, the 66-meter high towers already stood complete when it was decided to bring them together, and then to raise up the north tower. From 1399 to 1439, Jean Hülz of Cologne topped off the same tower with a majestic steeple, making for a total height of 142 meters.

The façade includes three portals adorned with a sumptuous display of statuary. The right portal depicts the parable of the wise virgins and the foolish virgins; on the left portal, the virtues are shown laying low the vices. There is a magnificent rose window 15 meters in diameter above the central portal, which is bordered by 10 statues of the Prophets. The spandrel depicts the New Testament. Above it, there is a double gable where the statues of King Solomon, the Virgin with Child, and the head of God the Father are to be found. The twelve lions symbolizing the tribes of Israel grace the stairs.

On the south side, the statues of women framing the

Southern transept and romanesque portal with clock (13th-century). Between the two doors is a statue of King Solomon rendering his verdict. On each side, the allegory of the proud and powerful church (left) and the sad and enfeebled synagogue (right). The blindfolded eyes symbolise error (right). Originals are in the Notre-Dame Paris Hall Museum.

Strasbourg Cathedral. Angel Pillar: a masterpiece of gothic sculpture at its height (circa 1235).

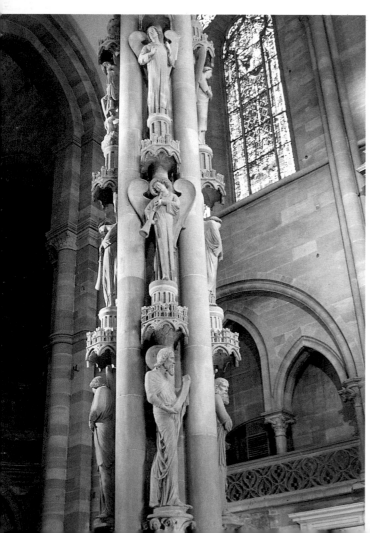

The organ-chest: loft and large console date from 1385, while the large organ built in the 15th century by Frédéric Krebs was completed by André Silbermann in 1716.

Carolingian stained glass window (north wall of the nave) from the 13th century.

Large stained glass window in the apse, the Virgin protecting the City, done by Max Ingrand in 1956 and donated by the members of the Council of Europe.

Strasbourg cathedral.

Right portal.
On the left, the tempter offers an apple to the boldest of the Mad Virgins. The filthy animals behind her back symbolise vice. But the Mad Virgins are tempted by superficial appearances, and are thus ready to sin.

Cathedral. Triptych (detail): Saint Maurice between Saints Nicolas, Roch, Matthew and Florian.

Cathedral, tympanum of the central portal illustrating the New Testament.

Right portal. On the right, the second part of the parable. Christ presents himself to the Wise Virgins who are ready to accept Him.

two Romanesque doors of the portal of the Clock (13th c.) represent the Church and the Synagogue. They are in fact copies; the originals can be seen in the Musée de l'Oeuvre Notre-Dame. In the middle, the statue of King Solomon, together with that of the Virgin Mary, overhanging the portal, date from the 19th century. The spandrel tells the story of the dormition of the Virgin Mary.

The portal on the left side dates from the 15th century. Restored in the 19th century, it recounts the martyrdom of Saint Lawrence.

Inside, the size of the cathedral is imposing: 103 meters long, the central nave — with seven bays — is 32 meters high and 16.4 meters wide. It opens into a 9-meter narthex. The stained glass windows date for the most part from the 13th and 14th centuries and recount in some 4,600 panels composed of 500,000 elements the secular history of the building and the city: from the New Testament along the south side-aisle, to the kings and emperors along the north side-aisle, to the Virgin, protectress of the city, in the apse, a modern work by Max Ingrand

Tympanum of right portal.

Central porch.

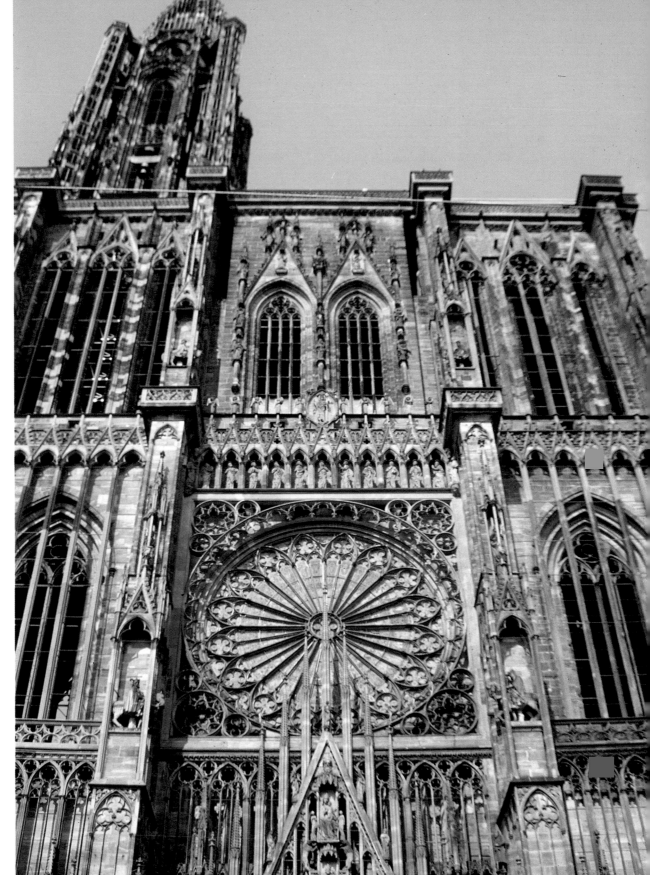

Western façade of the cathedral. Erwin de Steinbach supervised construction of this façade to a point just above the Apostles' Gallery over the rose window.

donated by the Council of Europe in 1956. Of particular interest where the furnishings are concerned is the pulpit (15th c.) and the great organ (1385 to 1716).

The two bays of the nave leading to the transept house, on the sides, the Saint Catherine (14th c.) and Saint Lawrence (16th c.) chapels, on the right and left, respectively. The left wing of the transept contains the baptismal font (1453), and a stone group showing Jesus on the Mount of Olives (1494) is contiguous to the Saint John the Baptist chapel (13th c.) and the tomb of the Bishop of Lichtenberg and the entrance to the Romanesque crypt. In the middle of the right wing of the transept, the column of the angels or the final judgement rises up in perfect Gothic harmony. The vaulting of the ribs is supported by an arrangement of eight ornate columns of three rows of four statues: Evangelists, deacons with trumpets, and Christ with three angels carrying the instruments of His passiosn. The Astronomical Clock (16th c.) was built on the basis of calculations by the mathematician Dasypodius and his team, the technical virtuosity of the Habrecht brothers (watchmakers), and the artistic deftness of Tobias Stimmer. The works needed to be refurbished between 1838 and 1842 by J.B. Schwilgué.

NOTRE-DAME PARISH HALL (LA MAISON DE L'ŒUVRE) AND MUSEUM

Formerly a Medieval institution responsibi-le for collecting the funds needed to build the cathedral, the parish hall is composed of two different buildings connected by wooden galleries on two levels.
The building on the left is Gothic (1347), while the one on the right is Renaissance (1579). A superb

Cathedral. Astronomical clock. Every quarter hour, Christ banishes Death; the first quarter is struck by the Infant, the second by the Adolescent, the third by Man, and the fourth by the Elder. The hours are rung by Death. On the last stroke, an angel turns the hourglass over. At 12.30 (the clock being half an hour slow), the Apostles file past Christ who then turns to the crowd and blesses it.

The cathedral steeple extending above the roofs typical of the old city houses.

Mercière Street seen from the top of the cathedral.

The twin towers of Notre-Dame Cathedral, whose steeple reaches 142 metres into the sky over Strasbourg.

spiral staircase rises between the two, at the back of the courtyard. In the center of it all is planted a small garden of vegetables and medicinal plants.

The current Museum includes the ancient Hôtellerie du Cerf as well the Parish buildings. Up until 1931, the Hostelry contained only the cathedral's fine original sculptures, as well as the architectural drawings and plans relating to the construction of the cathedral. Today, the Museum also shows the general artistic and cultural development of Strasbourg and Alsace. It offers fine collections of sculpture, stained glass, furniture, and gold and silver-ware, as well as painting (Schongauer, Hans Baldung-Grien, Stoskopff, Konrad Witz...).

ROHAN PALACE

This 18th-century French architectural ensemble is composed of buildings flanking a main courtyard at the back of which rises a fine classic façade with central pediment. The main façade gives onto a terrace on the banks of the Ill River. The Corinthian columns in the centre are a sign of the pure classicism of its style.

The princely residence of Strasbourg's bishops, this château was built between 1731 and 1744 by Massol, on plans by Robert de Cotte, for Cardinal Rohan-Soubise, the Bishop-Prince whose family occupied the episcopal see during the entire 18th-century.

It became part of the city museum system in 1898. Most of its interior decor has been preserved, notably the royal apartments used by Louis XV in 1744 and by Marie-Antoinette in 1770, as well as the bedroom and library used by the Rohan cardinals.

It houses the Museum of Fine Arts (large collection

of ancient and modern paintings, notably primitives and Renaissance painters, the Spanish, Dutch and French Schools as well as the Alsatian School — whose centerpiece is ''La Belle Strasbourgeoise'' by the Paris Master Nicolas de Largillière, 1703). It also includes the Museum of Decorative Arts (famous collection of fine ceramics and porcelain produced in Strasbourg by Hannong and de Niderviller, clocks, iron-work, etc.), the Archeological Museum (regional antiquities from the prehistoric period up to the major invasions), and the Print Collection (25,000 drawings and engravings, 40,000 volumes).

In summer, the main courtyard is the site of performances of traditional music and dance.

Rohan Palace. Main façade on the bank of the Ill. The pier for river launches.

Rohan Palace. Coat of Arms of the Rohan Bishop-Princes.

Traditional dances in the main courtyard of the palace.

Kammerzell House in Strasbourg was built from 1586 to 1589 for the merchant Martin Braun on top of a ground floor dating from 1467. This Alsatian Renaissance building is characterised by its extraordinary carved wood. The interior frescoes are the work of the Strasbourg painter Léo Schnugg (1878-1933).

Kammerzell House. Detail of carved beam.

KAMMERZELL HOUSE

Built over a ground floor dating from 1467, this house was constructed between 1586 and 1589 for a rich merchant named Martin Braun. The house changed hands several times, always remaining a shop, until the day when the spice merchant Kammerzell sold it to the Parish of Notre-Dame.

The building is remarkable for its carved half-timbering and beams illustrating the virtues, the senses, the zodiac, and the crafts, as well as classical and Christian heroes. The interior frescoes are the work of the Strasbourg painter Léon Schnugg (1878-1933).

RUE MERCIERE AND THE PHARMACIE DU CERF

The street just opposite the cathedral, *la rue Mercière,* evokes the city's medieval past. At the end of the street is one of the oldest pharmacies in Europe, the *pharmacie du cerf* (1262). It was rebuilt in the 15th century and completed in 1567.

SUCKLING-PIG MARKET SQUARE
(PLACE DU MARCHE-AUX-COCHONS-DE-LAIT)

This is the former marketplace for, precisely, suckling pigs. The square is flanked by houses dating from the 12th and 13th centuries. N. 1, a balconied residence topped by a weathervane in the form of a wooden clog, was built in 1602.

Deer's Pharmacie.

Suckling-Pig Market Square, yesterday and today.

Historical Museum, or "The Big Butcher's".

Raven Court. ▷

HISTORICAL MUSEUM

The museum has been housed in this former municipal slaughterhouse —known as "The Big Butcher's" (1587)— since 1919. It traces the city's political, topographic and military history.
Of notable interest is a relief map dating from 1727 which reproduces the city on a scale of 1/600 in surprising detail. There are also collections of traditional weapons and uniforms, not to mention the small painted cardboard soldiers which have been a Strasbourg specialty since before the Revolution.

RAVEN COURT *(COUR DU CORBEAU)*

Such illustrious guests as Turenne (1647), Jean Casimir, king of Poland (1668), Frederick II of Prussia (1740), Emperor Joseph II of Austria (1777) and Voltaire have stayed in this famous 16th century "Hostelry" located at 1, Quai des Bateliers. It boats

a fine inner courtyard from the 14th century with a well (1560). Two wooden galleries and octagonal tower enclosing a winding staircase lead to the guest rooms.

RAVEN BRIDGE *(PONT DU CORBEAU)*

Formerly called the "Bridge of Agony", this was where those sentenced to death were shut in a cage and drowned in the Ill.

ALSATIAN MUSEUM

This museum, which was opened in 1902 within three 16th and 17th-century Alsatian houses on the Quai St. Nicolas, recounts the lifestyle of the Alsace of yore. Popular arts, traditions and folklore are combined with substantial documentation on rural and artisanal life in the past.

Ancienne Douane

Musée alsacien

Raven
Bridge and
the Old
Customs
House
(Museum of
Modern
Art).

Typical
signs for
the Old
Customs
House and
the Alsatian
Museum.

Alsatian
Museum.

MUSEE
ALSACIEN

OLD CUSTOMS HOUSE *(L'ANCIENNE DOUANE)* — MUSEUM OF MODERN ART

The old customs house (1358) —called the "Kaufhaus" in the 14th century—, was originally the warehouse for the city's river trade. Enlarged several times in the 16th and 18th centuries, almost completely destroyed in 1944 and rebuilt in 1965, this building today houses the Collection of Alsatian Art and the Museum of Modern Art.

It contains work by Impressionist artists (Boudin, Monet, Degas, Renoir, Pissarro...) and 20th-century artists (Dufy, Maillol, Lurçat, Braque...). The foremost painting is indisputably "The Kiss" (1910) by the Austrian painter Gustav Klimt. The museum is also proud of the room devoted to drawings by the Strasbourg artist Hans Arp (1877-1966), who was one of the founders of the Dada movement. The attic floor shows off stained glass produced from 1900 to the present.

Statue and Gutenberg Square.

St. Thomas' Church.

GUTENBERG SQUARE

Known as the ''Herb Market'' up to 1781, this was the city's economic and administrative centre. The Town Hall *(Hôtel de Ville)* or ''Pfalz'' was located there, as was the Mint *(Hôtel de la Monnaie)*, built in 1582 under the influence of the Italian Renaissance and today housing the Trade Hall *(Hôtel de Commerce)*.

In the centre of the square is a bronze statue of Gutenberg sculpted by David d'Angers in 1840 on the occasion of the 400th anniversary of the invention of moveable type. It was in fact in Strasbourg that Gutenberg, having fled his native Mayence for political reasons, lived from 1434 to 1438 and where he collaborated with three Alsatians to refine various ''secret processes'' which he had invented.

SAINT-THOMAS' CHURCH

Founded at the end of the 7th century by St. Florent, Bishop of Strasbourg, it became a collegiate church in the 11th century, and joined the Reformation in 1549. It remains a Protestant church today.

Inside can be found the famous mausoleum (1756-1777) of the Maréchal de Saxe (died 1750), a masterwork by Pigalle commissioned by Louis XV. Mozart (1778) and Schweitzer played the Silbermann organ.

Mausoleum of the Maréchal de Saxe: France, weeping, holds the Field Marshal's hand and tries to fend off Death who is lifting the lid of the tomb. Strength (Hercules) and Love are given to grief. The Lion (Holland), Leopard (England), and Eagle (Austria) are thrown back, defeated, onto their crumpled flags.

*Typical houses near
Saint Martin bridge.*

*Evening concert -
Benjamin Zix Square.*

A ''Winstub''.

LA PETITE FRANCE

In the Middle Ages, this was the neighbourhood of the tanning, milling and fishing guilds. Its name comes from a house called ''Zum Franzölel'' in the local language. Soldiers from Charles VIII's Italian expedition were treated for their ''maladies'' there in 1867.

One of the most picturesque and best preserved sections of old Strasbourg, *La Petite France* (''Little France'') retains its charm and offers a captivating atmosphere at day's end. The fine Alsatian Renaissance houses are enchanting with their overhanging floors, their carved wooden timbers, balconies, gables and large sloping roofs designed for drying skins. Not to mention wonderful reflections in the canal, the ''winstubs'' where it's so pleasant to try a small pitcher of local wine, or the shaded alleyways such as *la rue du Bain-aux-plantes* flanked by magnificent 16th and 17th-century houses (notably Nos. 42 —the Tanners' House, 1572— 33, 31, 27 and 25 (1651).

A stall on the Rue du Bain-aux-Plantes.

The charm of ''Petite
France''.
The Tanners' House.
The banks of the Ill.

Rue du
Bain-aux-
Plantes. ▷

"Petite France". In the background are the cathedral and St. Thomas' Church (about 1860).

THE COVERED BRIDGES

In the 13th century, wooden bridges linked three large, square towers which were part of the city's defense against marauding barons and pillaging hordes. From the 16th century up to 1784, the bridges were covered with sloping roofs. No longer existant, these were rebuilt in stone from 1860 to 1870. The three towers, as well as a fourth situated at the end of Turckheim Quay, are vestiges of the ancient fortifications. The row of bridges spans four of the Ill River.

VAUBAN DAM

A fortified bridge built by Vauban (the remains of Vauban's defensive walls), it is composed of three arches and is called "the big lock" because is controls the flow of the Ill. Today transformed into a terrace with panoramic view, it offers a magnificent view of the Covered Bridges and four Towers, the Petite France area with its canals, and the cathedral in the distance. Statues and architectural fragments from the city's churches are displayed on the ground floor.

◁ *The banks of the Ill (pages 40/41).*

The covered bridges.

Vauban Dam.

The atmosphere along
the banks of the Ill.

Kléber Square. The cathedral and New Temple are in the background.

Church of St.-Pierre-Le-Jeune.

KLEBER SQUARE

Formerly the military paradeground, this square harbours the statue erected in 1840 to Imperial General Kléber (born March 9, 1753 in Strasbourg, assassinated in Cairo on June 14, 1800). His ashes repose in a vault under the pedestal. Two bas-reliefs recall his victories at Altenkirchen and Heliopolis. The square is bounded on the north by a building known as the *Aubette* ("Dawn Inn"), a former garrison built by Blondel from 1765 to 1771. It owes its name to the fact that sentry passwords and instructions were give to the soldiers at dawn *(l'aube).*

MAN OF IRON SQUARE
(PLACE DE L'HOMME DE FER)

This square owes its name to an 18th-century weapons shop formerly at No. 2. The shop's sign was a full-sized dummy dressed in the 16th-century armour of a sergeant of the municipal guard. The pharmacy which replaced the weapons dealer in 1870 is still there, along with a copy of the armour, the original armour now being preserved in the Historical Museum.

CHURCH OF ST.-PIERRE-LE-JEUNE

This former Irish monastery (founded in the 7th century) is now a Protestant church. The original Romanesque church was consecrated by Pope Leo IX in 1053. The current church was begun in 1250 with the construction of the nave and choir. It was completed in 1320 and restored in 1894. The interior houses an admirable 14th-century rood-

The sign of the Man of Iron.

Broglie Square - Town Hall.

screen and a Silbermann organ. To the north of the church is an ancient cloister; three of its galleries date from the 11th 12tht centuries, and the fourth from the 14th century. There are also tombstones and inscriptions from the 14th and 16th centuries.

BROGLIE SQUARE

This former "Horse Market" was transformed into a public promenade in 1740 by Field Marshal Broglie, governor of Alsace in 1739-1743. The Town Hall *(Hôtel de Ville)* was built there from 1730 to 1736 by Massol as the mansion of the Counts of Hanau-Lichtenberg. At one end is the Opera-Theatre (1804-1825) which was rebuilt after the bombardment of 1870. It sports columns and muses sculpted by Ohmacht (1820). The monument to Field Marshal Leclerc is placed in the centre of the square. Leclerc had vowed to raise the French flag over Strasbourg Cathedral, and his 2nd Armoured Division liberated Strasbourg on November 23, 1944. At No. 4 (currently the Bank of France), a plaque notes that in this house (that of Frédéric de Diétrich, the first constitutional Mayor of Strasbourg) Rouget de l'Isle first sang his battle song composed for the Army of the Rhine, on April 25, 1792. The song was later adopted as the national anthem, "La Marseillaise". The house was also the birthplace of the missionary Charles de Foucauld (September 15, 1858).

Memorial to General Leclerc and the Municipal Theatre (Opera).

PREFECTURE

Situated on Broglie Square, the Prefecture was built by François Joseph Klinghin, King's Representative to the Court of Justice, in 1736. The building also served as the House of the Royal Administrator until 1790, as well as that of the Departmental Prefect from 1871 to 1918.

Prefecture Building.

*Municipal
Theatre
(Opera),
Broglie
Square.*

*National
Library
(1895),
Place de la
République.*

National Theatre of Strasbourg.

Sculling on the Ill.

Aerial view of the Place de la République.

NORTH-EAST SECTOR, 19TH CENTURY

When Alsace became part of Germany in 1870, a new "German" city was built to the north-east, deliberately separate from the old city and including the University and the Orangery.

It represented an affirmation of a new contribution to the city's culture. Numerous monumental public buildings line wide roads, today providing a rare example of Prussian architecture in the Gothic-Renaissance style. Following the city's postwar expansion, this neighbourhood now forms an integral part of Strasbourg's urban fabric.

PLACE DE LA REPUBLIQUE

Formerly the *Kaiser Platz* ("Imperial Square"), it became *La Place de la République* ("Republic Square") when France reclaimed Alsace-Lorraine in 1918.

This geometric square is bounded on the east by the Music Conservatory (1892), the Strasbourg National Theatre, and the National Library (1895). On the north side are the Prefecture's administrative offices, with the Rhine Palace (1888) on the west. In the centre of the square is a round tree-lined garden in which is found the 1914-1918 war monument sculpted by Drivier in 1936.

RHINE PALACE

This former Imperial Palace, built for Wilhelm II when in residence in Strasbourg, was constructed from 1883 to 1888 by Hermann Hebert on the model of public buildings in Berlin. The colossal and triumphant proportions of its architecture harks back the Italian Renaissance. Today it houses various cultural organisations.

Rhine Palace, Place de la République (1888).

Synagogue de la Paix
(1955).

St. Paul's Church
(1892) at the junction
of the Ill and the Aar.

University Hall (1885).

CONTADES PARK

Located to the north of Place de la République, this park was named after Field Marshal Contades, who was named military governor of Alsace in 1762 in Strasbourg. Known as a gourmet, he enjoyed treating his guests and hired a young cook named Jean-Pierre Clause in 1778. In an effort to outdo himself, Clause invented a specialty which, thanks to Alsatian geese, would conquer the world. It involves a firm and smooth goose liver pâté surrounded by finelly chopped veal and bacon, covered in a pastry crust cooked till golden in a low oven.

SYNAGOGUE DE LA PAIX

Built in 1955 to replace the one destroyed in 1940, this "Synagogue of Peace" is an impressive yet harmonious building on the edge of Contades Park.

SAINT-PAUL'S CHURCH

This Protestant church is a fine, twin-steepled building in the early ogival style (1889-1892), at the junction of the Ill and Aar Rivers.

UNIVERSITY HALL *(PALAIS DE L'UNIVERSITE)*

This 1885 Italian Renaissance Revival building is an important research centre and institute, combining seven schools within the university of which Goethe was unquestionably the most famous student. A monument to his memory stands in the square amidst flowerbeds and fountains. Behind the university are the Botanical Gardens, the Zoological Museum, and the Planetarium.

GOETHE IN STRASBOURG

Goethe (1749-1832) studied law at the University of Strasbourg in 1770. He resided in a family boarding house on the Rue du Vieux-Marché-aux-Poissons. To overcome his vertigo, he is said to have climbed to the top ot the cathedral tower as a test of will. He had a passing affair with Frédérique, daughter of the pastor of Sessenheim, to which he later referred in his memoires.
He also undertook research leading to the rediscovery

Statue of Goethe.

House where Goethe lived.

Joséphine Pavilion (1805).

of the tomb of Erwin, the artist responsible for the façade of the cathedral. After receiving his Doctor of Law degree on August 6, 1771, Goethe returned to Frankfurt.

ORANGERY PARK

This beautiful park was laid out by Le Nôtre in 1692, and was redone in 1804 for the visit of the Empress Joséphine. Boudhors erected the Joséphine Pavilion there in 1805. It burned in 1968, was rebuilt, and is now used for concerts, plays, and exhibitions. During the Universal Exposition of 1900, an old Alsatian half-timbered farmhouse dating from 1608 was dismantled and transfered to the park. Called the Buerehiesel, it serves as a restaurant. A lake and zoo are additional features of this fine park.

Orangery Park - French gardens laid out by Le Nôtre.
The Buerehiesel - The zoo - The lake.

General view of the Palace of Europe and the European Court of Human Rights.

PALACE OF EUROPE

Henri Bernard's boldly modern architecture rises opposite Orangery Park. Inaugurated in January 1977, it took over from the smaller buildings remodelled in 1950. The Palace houses the Council of Europe which counts 21 member countries. Since its creation in July 1949, the European Parliament has met in Strasbourg; members are now elected by direct universal suffrage. The European Court of Human Rights adjoins the Palace of Europe, and these two institutions contain the seeds of Europe in the third millenium.

MUSIC AND CONFERENCE HALL (PALAIS DE LA MUSIQUE ET DES CONGRES)

In the midst of a green 16-acre site, this hall was opened in 1975 and offers advanced audio-visual and communications facilities in an outstandingly beautiful architectural setting.

Conference Hall -
The banks of the Rhine -
The border post on Europe Bridge.

Sunset.

Contents

POTENTIAL ITINERARIES

One-Day Visit

Cathedral - Notre-Dame Parish Hall Museum - Rohan Palace - Petite France - (Rue du Bain-aux-Plantes) - Old houses on Broglie Square (Rue Brûlée).

Two-Day visit

Cathedral - Notre-Dame Parish Hall Museum - Rohan Palace - Historical Museum, St. Thomas' Church - Petite France (Rue du Bain-aux-Plantes) - Covered Bridges - Old houses on Broglie Square (Rue Brûlée) - Place de la République - University Campus.

Three or more days

Discover the city yourself by using the list of contents opposite and then leafing through this booklet. You may also want to refer to the guide *Vision and comprehension of Alsace and the Upper Vosges* by the same publisher.

Some of you will have lots of time to stroll through the streets, visit monuments and museums, and meet the people of Strasbourg. Others will have less time, and some may have none at all. Whatever the case, the publisher hopes that this series of images will help you to discover, understand and retain pleasant memories of the spirit and charm of Strasbourg.

Back cover: Kammezell House.